How Did Bill Gates Get His First Million?

Biography of Famous People Children's Biography Books

Speedy Publishing LLC
40 E. Main St. #1156
Newark, DE 19711
www.speedypublishing.com

In this book, we're going to talk about the life of billionaire entrepreneur Bill Gates. So let's get right to it!

WHO IS BILL GATES?

Bill Gates is a famous entrepreneur who is an innovator in the field of technology and a very smart business strategist. With his business partner, Paul Allen, he built an enormous, highly profitable software business called Microsoft.

Microsoft Windows.

EARLY LIFE

Born on October 28, 1955, Bill was the middle child of an important Seattle lawyer named William H. Gates II and a teacher turned homemaker, Mary Maxwell Gates. His parents met at the University of Washington when his father was a shy, intelligent law student and his mother was an athlete and a student leader.

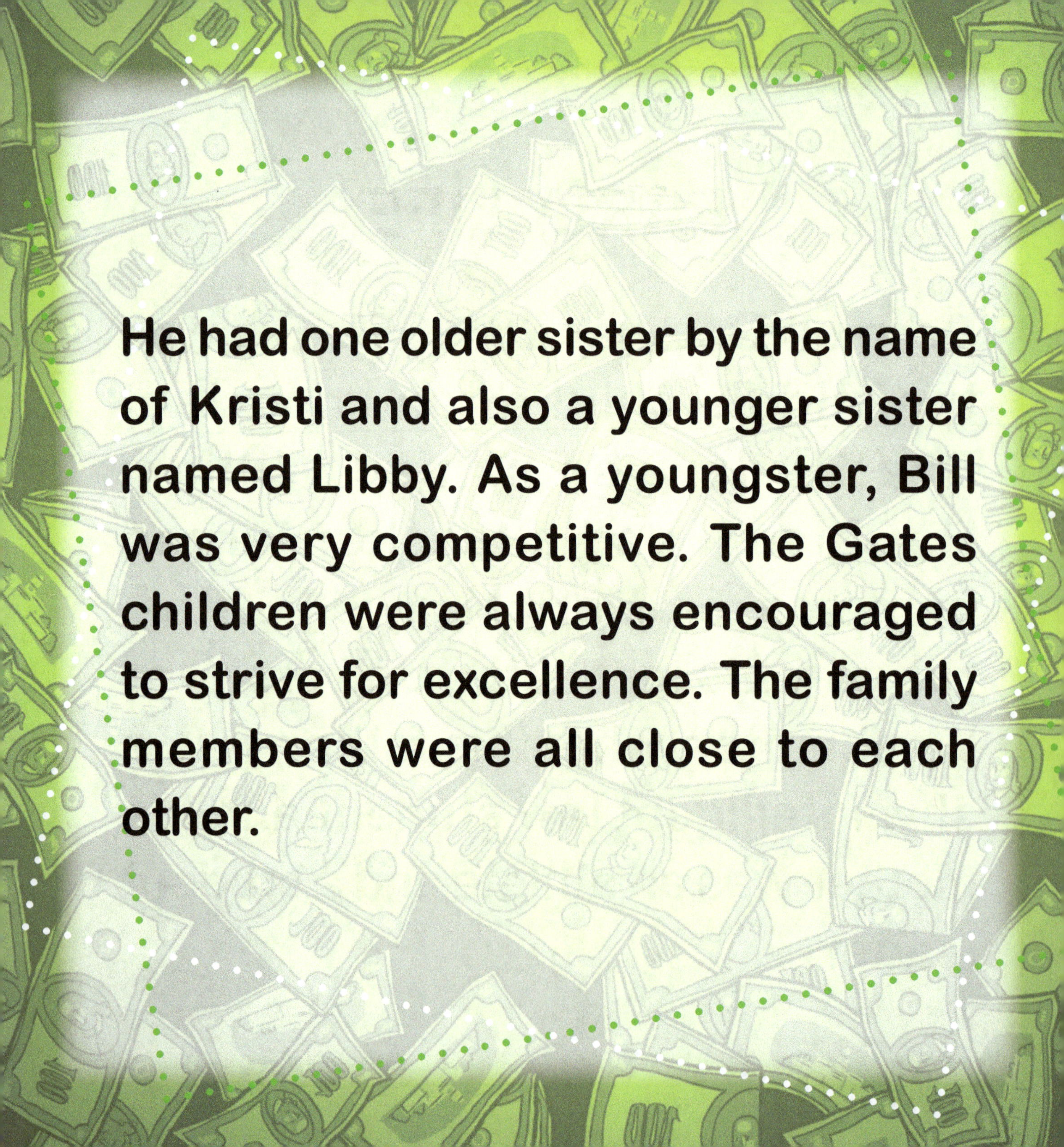

He had one older sister by the name of Kristi and also a younger sister named Libby. As a youngster, Bill was very competitive. The Gates children were always encouraged to strive for excellence. The family members were all close to each other.

Bill was exceptionally good at board games like Monopoly and he excelled at math. He was very bored in school and sometimes got into trouble since he wasn't challenged enough. His parents encouraged him to pursue extracurricular activities to keep him interested. He was an avid reader and loved science fiction books. He also did well in Boy Scouts.

When Bill became a teenager, his parents sent him to the prestigious Lakeside Preparatory School. They were hoping that this new, more challenging, school would keep him engaged. It was at Lakeside where he was introduced to his future business associate Paul Allen. He was also able to work with computers. Both these events changed his life.

INTRODUCTION TO COMPUTERS

When Bill was a young man, there weren't any desktop computers, laptops or tablets like we have today. Computers were huge and sometimes filled up an entire room. They were so expensive that they were mostly owned by large companies.

DFID
Department for International Development
www.dfid.gov.uk

SURVIVAL SUPPLIES
TO DISPENSE:
TO REUSE AS COMMODE:

Bill's school purchased time so that the students could use the computer. Bill was absolutely fascinated by the computer. He started writing programs that the computer could use to do certain things. One of the first programs he wrote was for a computer game based on tic-tac-toe.

In fact, Bill and some of the other students at the school were so fascinated by the computer that they hacked into it so they could continue working when their time was up. They eventually offered to troubleshoot bugs for the company who owned the computer in exchange for more computer time.

While Bill was still in high school, he created a payroll program for yet another company as well as a scheduling program for his school. With his friend and business collaborator Paul Allen, he began a business program to track Seattle's traffic.

A DEAL WITH MITS

Bill went to Harvard after high school and pursued a course of study to become a lawyer like his dad. He was still intrigued by computers and spent a lot of time writing programs. He also kept connected to his friend Paul.

Microsoft

At that time, the idea of desktop computers was just starting. Ed Roberts, the head of a company that he founded called Micro Instrumentation and Telemetry Systems (MITS) had just created a kit to put together a home computer. The computer was called the Altair 8800 and it had been featured in a magazine called Popular Electronics.

Bill and Paul were very excited by the Altair 8800 and they decided that they could write a software program in the BASIC computing language that would run on the computer. It would be a form of BASIC designed just for the Altair computer to use. They called MITS and told them about it. They made it sound like they were already half finished with it, but Bill hadn't even started it yet!

When they went to New Mexico a month later, the software was completed and ran perfectly. They continued to work with MITS and created more software for the Altair. These were their first software programs for the company Bill and Paul would soon start, called Microsoft.

STARTING MICROSOFT

Bill dropped out of Harvard to start Microsoft with his friend Paul in 1975. The company's software was doing extremely well and they were making a lot of money. When Bill was in school, he had told his teachers he would be a millionaire by age 30, but by 1978 at the young age of 23, Bill was already a millionaire. More exciting events were ahead for Microsoft.

GAVI
ALLIANCE

The company was five years old when Bill made a deal with IBM that would change the world of computing forever. Microsoft had bought an operating system for the desktop personal computer that they called the Microsoft Disk Operating System or MS-DOS for short. At that time, International Business Machines, abbreviated as IBM, was on its way to becoming the largest computer company in the world.

They had developed a desktop personal computer or PC. Bill struck a deal with IBM. Microsoft would adapt the MS-DOS operating system to work on IBM's computers. IBM could use and package the MS-DOS operating system with their computers for a fee of 50 thousand dollars plus licensing fees for every software package that was sold with a PC.

IBM wanted to buy the program outright, but Bill would not agree. In a brilliant move that netted Microsoft billions of dollars, he kept the rights and was able to adapt the software for other computers as well. When other manufacturers started to make personal computers, they were also able to buy Microsoft's software. Within 10 years, Microsoft was the operating system installed on most computers worldwide.

MICROSOFT WINDOWS

Though Steve Jobs, the Founder of Apple Computers, and Bill were rivals, they actually shared many of their first innovations. In 1981 Apple invited Microsoft to create software that would work on Apple's Macintosh computers.

GATES

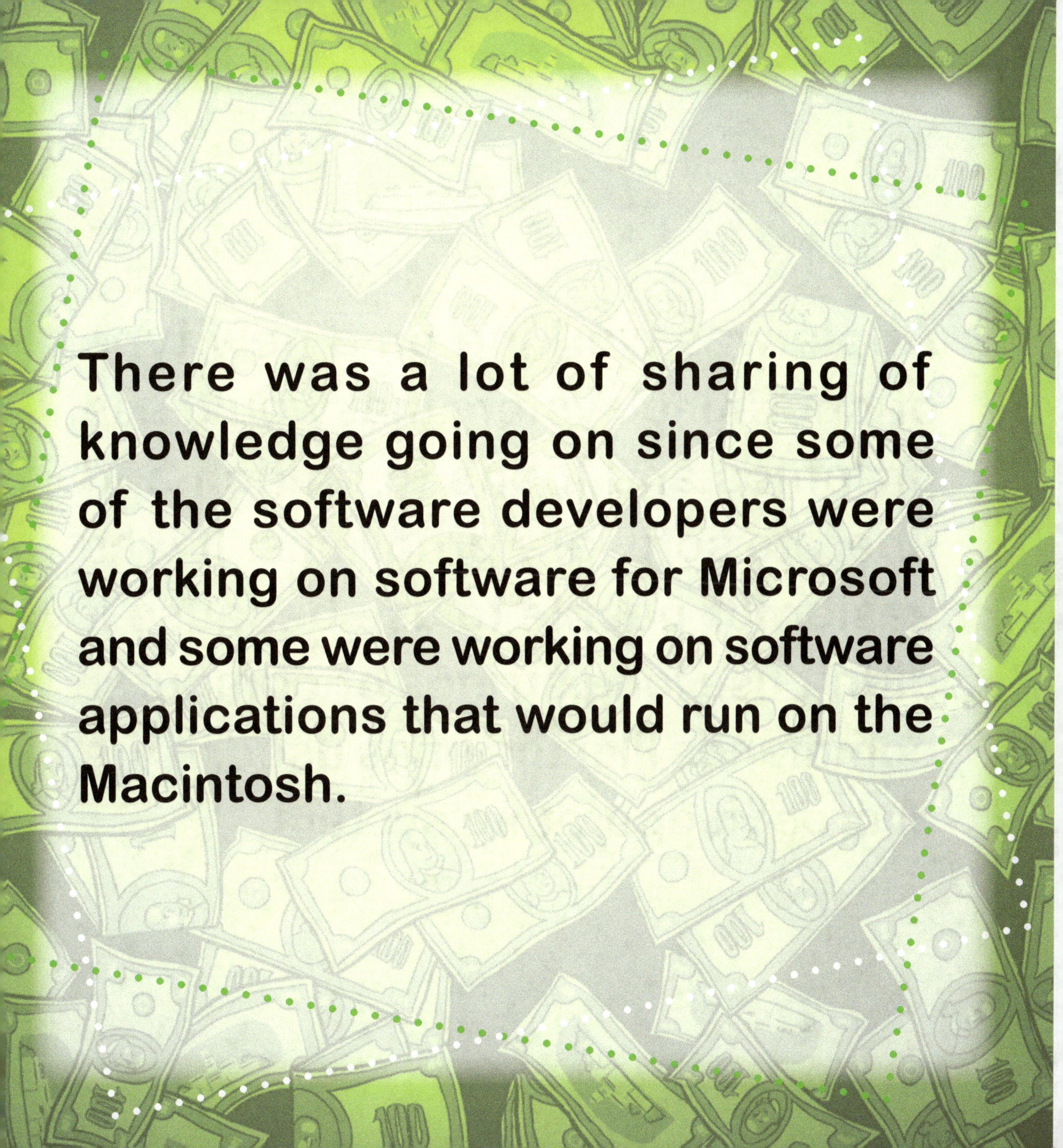

There was a lot of sharing of knowledge going on since some of the software developers were working on software for Microsoft and some were working on software applications that would run on the Macintosh.

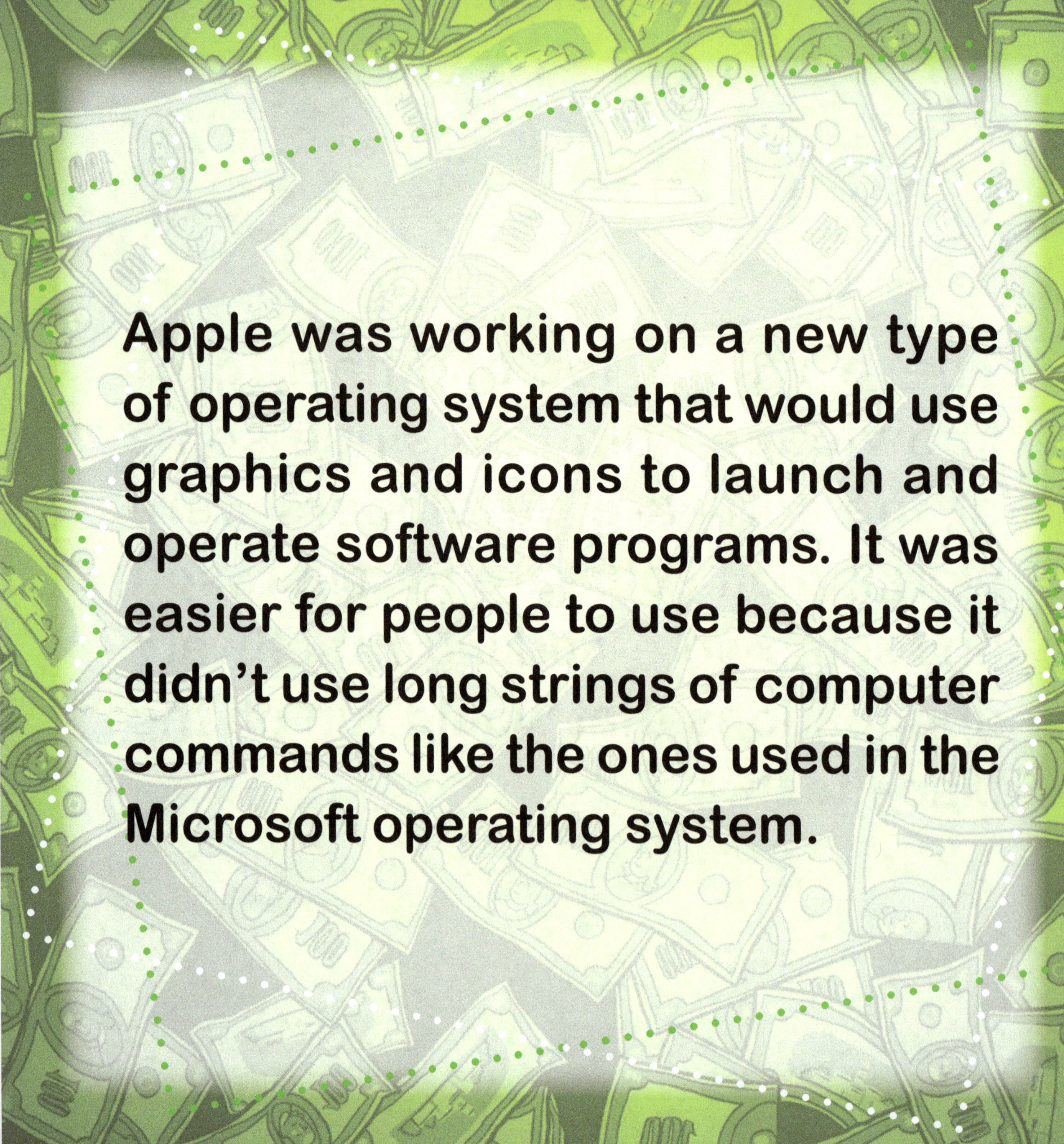

Apple was working on a new type of operating system that would use graphics and icons to launch and operate software programs. It was easier for people to use because it didn't use long strings of computer commands like the ones used in the Microsoft operating system.

Apple launched this new system that used a graphical user interface, called GUI, in 1984. Not to be outdone, Bill realized that this was a huge threat to his computer empire. He announced that there was soon going to be a new operating system called "Windows" and that it would work with all the software that MS-DOS users currently had.

The development of Windows hadn't yet started! In the year that followed, Microsoft developed the software. Rather than switch to a completely new way of running software, most PC users waited until Windows was ready and Microsoft kept their empire.

At the beginning some people complained that the Windows operating system wasn't as good as Apple's. However, Microsoft Windows, like the previous software from Microsoft, could run on all different types of PCs, while Apple's could only run on Apple's computers. Microsoft kept the operating system market and soon Windows was running on over 90% of the world's desktop computers.

FROM MILLIONS TO BILLIONS

In 1986, Bill offered stock in Microsoft. Once the company offered their stock on the stock exchange, the company was valued at $520 million dollars and Bill owned almost half of the stock. Microsoft continued to grow and its stock price increased rapidly. At one point, his stock was worth over $100 billion dollars and Bill Gates was the richest man on Earth.

GIVING WEALTH AWAY

After many years of dedication and hard work, Bill stepped away from the day-to-day work at Microsoft in June of 2008. It was his wife Melinda that got him interested in taking a more important role as a civic leader as his mother Mary had done before him. He started to think about his legacy and how he could support others through charitable work.

He began to turn his attention away from business while he and his wife discussed how they could change their lives. He turned the duties at Microsoft over to a college friend by the name of Steve Ballmer. Steve had been with the company since 1980 and he took over the position of CEO that was formerly Bill's job.

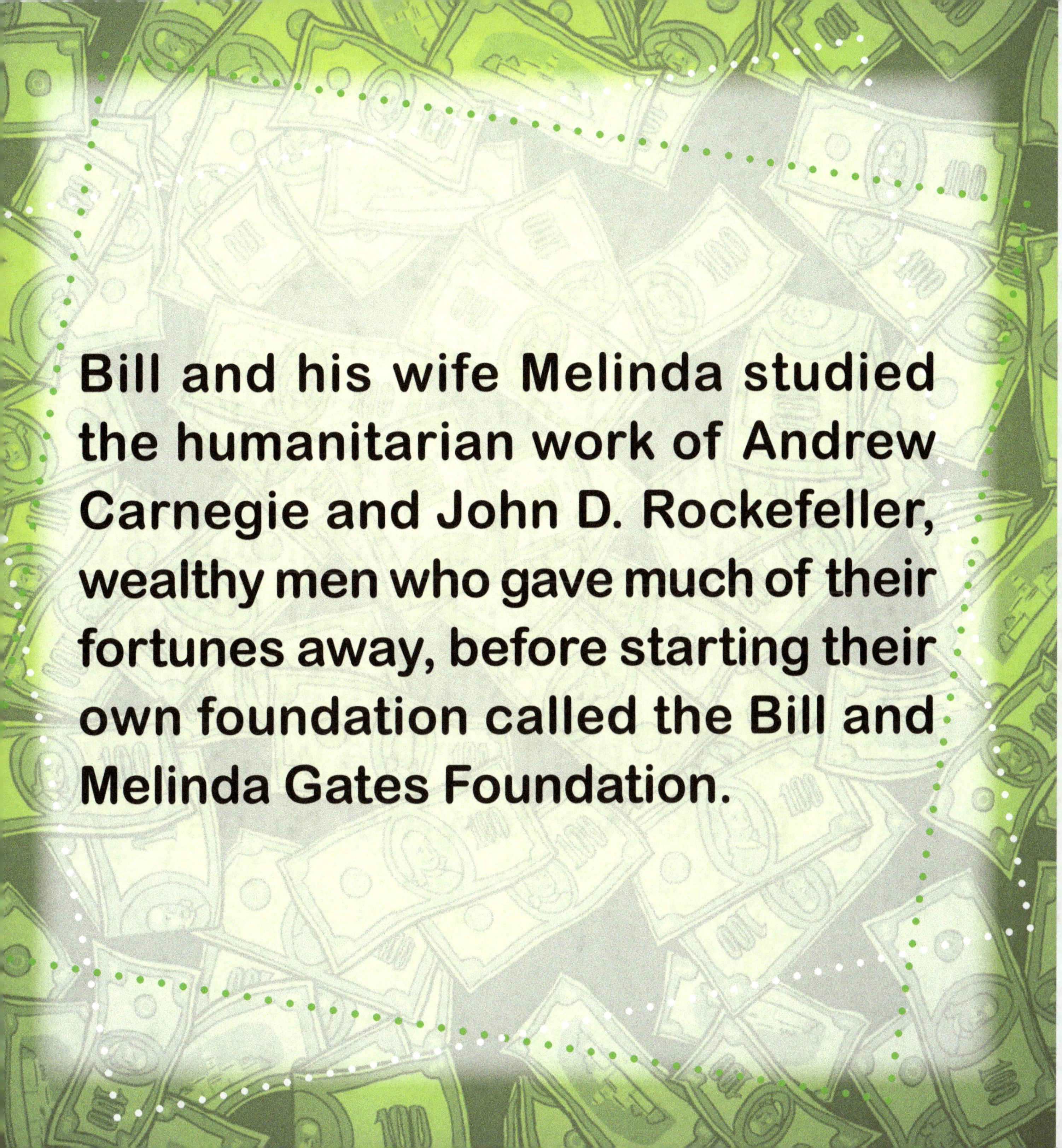

Bill and his wife Melinda studied the humanitarian work of Andrew Carnegie and John D. Rockefeller, wealthy men who gave much of their fortunes away, before starting their own foundation called the Bill and Melinda Gates Foundation.

They started the foundation with their own contribution of $28 billion dollars. Their foundation is dedicated to education for all and improving health for people throughout the world. In 2016, President Obama gave the Presidential Medal of Freedom to them for the work they have done worldwide to better humanity.

DFID Department for International Development

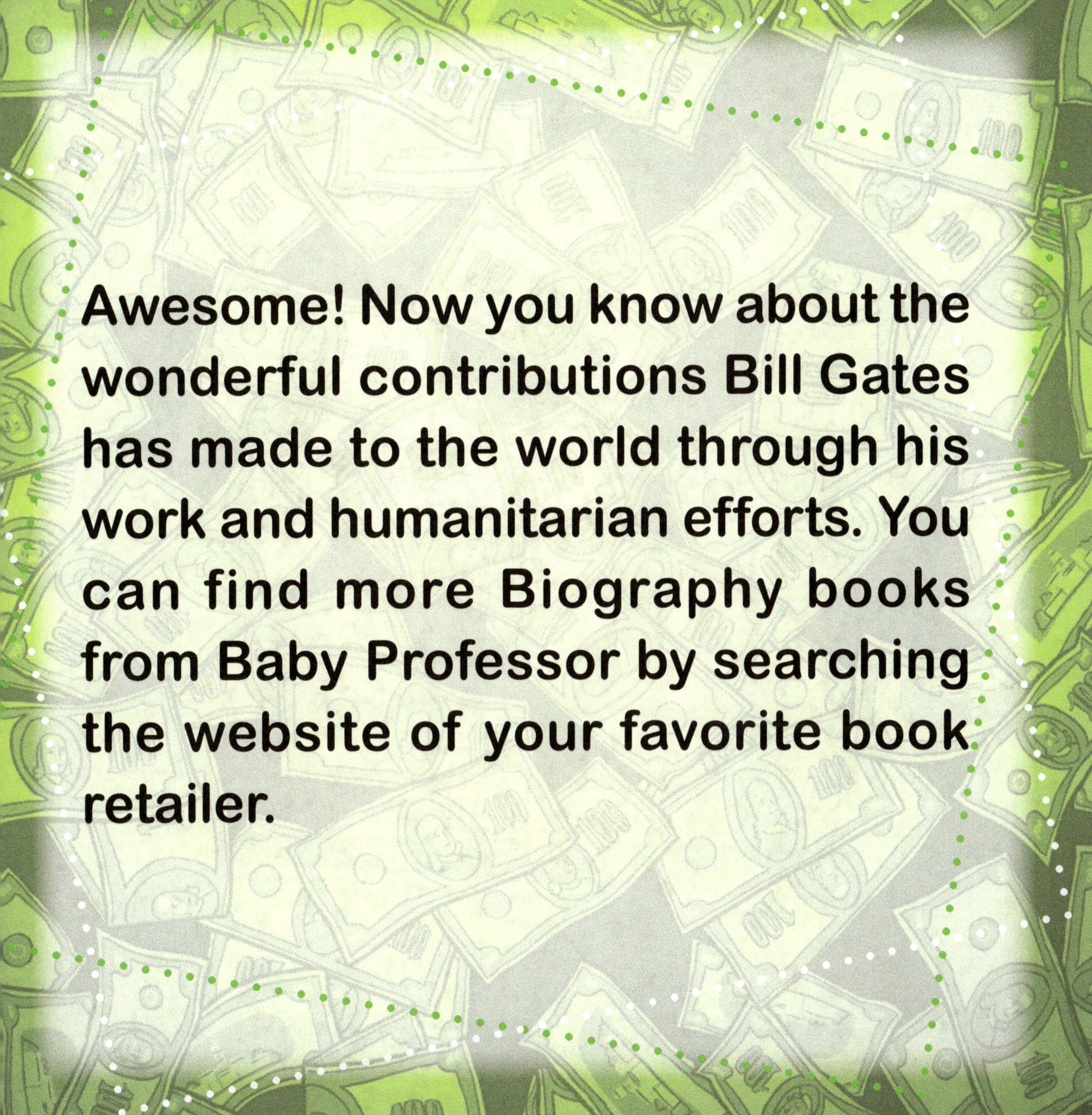

Awesome! Now you know about the wonderful contributions Bill Gates has made to the world through his work and humanitarian efforts. You can find more Biography books from Baby Professor by searching the website of your favorite book retailer.

Visit
BABY PROFESSOR
EDUCATION KIDS
www.BabyProfessorBooks.com
to download Free Baby Professor eBooks
and view our catalog of new and exciting
Children's Books

www.ingramcontent.com/pod-product-compliance
Lightning Source LLC
LaVergne TN
LVHW060827170826
845678LV00010B/1921
9798869438348